HOMESTYLE WOK COOKING
IN PICTURES

HOMESTYLE WOK COOKING IN PICTURES

Yung Ching Hsing

SHUFUNOTOMO/JAPAN PUBLICATIONS

© Copyright in Japan 1982 by Yung Ching Hsing
Illustrations by An Corporation
Photographs by Katsuhiko Ogawa and
                Shufunotomo Co., Ltd.
English text supervised by Linda Tierney

Paper Over Board Edition
First printing: September 1991

Published by SHUFUNOTOMO CO., LTD.
2–9, Kanda Surugadai, Chiyoda-ku, Tokyo, 101 Japan

Sole Overseas Distributor: Japan Publications Trading Co., Ltd.
P.O. Box 5030 Tokyo International, Tokyo, Japan
Distributors:
UNITED STATES: Kodansha America, Inc., through Farrar, Straus &
Giroux, 19 Union Square West, New York, NY 10003.
CANADA: Fitzhenry & Whiteside Ltd., 195 Allstate Parkway, Markham,
Ontario L3R 4T8.
BRITISH ISLES AND EUROPEAN CONTINENT: Premier Book Marketing Ltd.,
1 Gower Street, London WC1E 6HA.
AUSTRALIA AND NEW ZEALAND: Bookwise International,
54 Crittenden Road, Findon, South Australia 5023.
THE FAR EAST AND JAPAN: Japan Publications Trading Co., Ltd.,
1–2–1, Sarugaku-cho, Chiyoda-ku, Tokyo 101.

Library of Congress Catalog Card L/C No. 81–84805
ISBN 0–87040–510–1
Printed in Japan

Preface

When I was just a mere child, I would call morning greetings to my parents, pass through the sweet-smelling flowers and fruit-bearing trees in the front garden, and run into the yard at the rear of the house. Completely different from the peaceful fragrance of the front garden, the rear yard was busy and noisy with people working.

There were young male servants working in the vegetable gardens and maids hurrying around. There were gardens to be watered and animals to be fed. We kept many domestic animals such as carp, snapping turtles, chickens, ducks, turkeys and sometimes eels or pigs. My mother and the cook firmly believed that the best taste of produce and meat begins with good fertilizer and feed. The ingredients for our cooking were always fresh from the yard.

Amongst the servants worked a cook who was a wonderful storyteller. I was a constant guest in the kitchen, for I loved to hear his stories. I came to learn his secrets of cooking while watching him and listening to his tales.

Thinking back now, it seems to me that those days were the beginning of my love for home-style Chinese cooking. When I was older, I went on to school and studied music, but I returned to cooking in the end as I was so fond of it. Now I am more than pleased to share with you some of my favorite recipes.

One of our greatest responsibilities as homemakers is to promote the best health of our families through good food. The appropriate cooking utensils, the freshest and highest quality ingredients, mastery of the skills of cooking methods, and attractive serving dishes are all basic elements of good cooking. It is possible for every one of us to strive to meet these technical requirements, but let us not forget an old saying that "heart, love and sincerity" are the true essentials of cooking.

May you have a love of cooking and a great pride in serving delicious, nutritious dishes to your beloved families.

Yung-Ching Shing

Yung Ching Hsing

Contents

Cooking Utensils

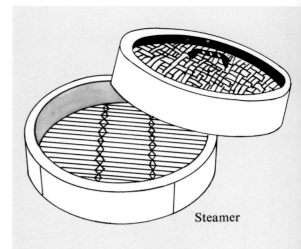

Steamer

Woks come in two styles: with one handle and with two handles. They also come in various sizes. The bigger the wok, the more even a temperature can be maintained. The diameter of the wok should be wider than the stove burner. A wok may be made of iron or of stainless steel coated with teflon. The disadvantage of the teflon coating is that it eventually chips and wears away. An iron wok darkens and improves with use.

A new wok must be treated to remove the rust preventative. Scrub wok with cleanser, rinse well and heat on the burner to dry. When dry, add enough oil to cover the surface and reheat. Turn off heat and let cool. Drain oil. Rinse with hot water and heat to dry. If any odor from the rust preventative remains, repeat this process.

Strainer
One handy utensil is a wide, flat, mesh strainer that fits into the wok. It can be used as a basket for cooking small or soft ingredients, or as a drainer.

It permits small ingredients to be evenly fried together for the same amount of time.

Ladle
The curved ladle is used for spooning liquids and as a spatula. A ladle should have a long handle for safety. A netted ladle is convenient for spooning noodles and vegetables.

Steamer
The steamer, whether made of bamboo or aluminum, fits into the wok. Steam from the boiling water in the wok rises through the steamer to cook the food. The steamer should have two or more layers and a lid. Each layer can be used to cook a separate dish at the same time. The small-sized steamer can be used for serving as well as cooking.

After each use, a bamboo steamer should be washed and thoroughly air-dried.

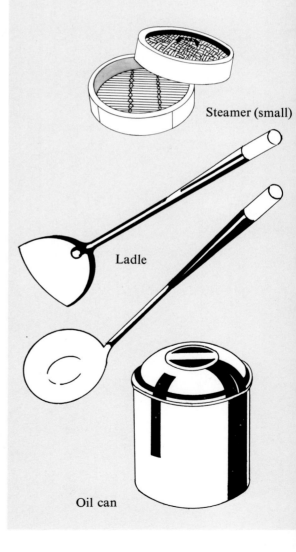

Steamer (small)

Ladle

Oil can

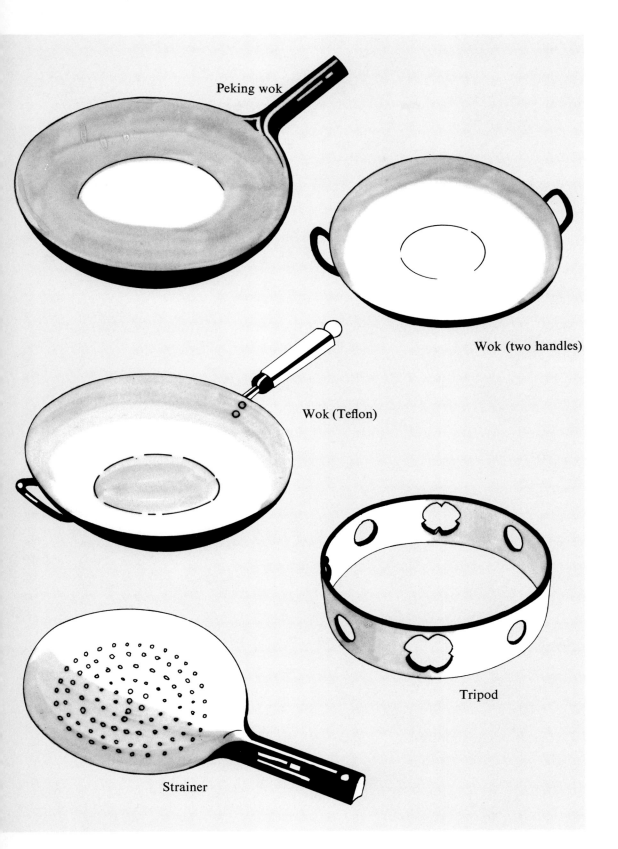

Peking wok

Wok (two handles)

Wok (Teflon)

Tripod

Strainer

9

Oils and Cooking Methods

Oils

Oils are basic ingredients in many Chinese recipes, are used in cooking, and as a seasoning.

Lard is the traditionally favored Chinese cooking oil, but today it is known to be less desirable because of its high cholesterol content. Such vegetable oils as peanut, corn, or safflower are low in cholesterol and are good substitutes for lard. Peanut oil is especially good when cooking is done at high temperatures, because it has a low burning and smoking point. Fats such as Crisco, which tend to solidify when cool, are not suitable.

Sesame oil is often sprinkled sparingly on a dish before serving or in a sauce to add flavor. It is best to buy sesame oil in small amounts and to replace the bottle top immediately, as it quickly and easily loses its flavor when exposed to air.

How Oil Can Be Recycled

Cooking oil can be strained to remove lingering taste and odor and used again. You will need a coffee can or steel container about 6 inches (15 cm) in diameter, a strainer that fits the can, and paper towels. Line strainer with 2–3 paper towels and place on can. Pour hot oil (you may need to reheat the oil that has cooled since it was used earlier) through paper towels. Discard paper towels. Let oil cool. Cover and store in the refrigerator.

Deep-Frying Preparation

Deep-fried foods are fried in several inches of oil at a high, constant temperature. The foods will be crispy on the outside and tender and moist inside.

Deep-Frying

Heat wok over low heat for about 1 minute. Add oil and heat over high heat for 5 to 10 minutes. For 4–5 servings, 2–3 cups of oil are adequate. Ingredients without a batter are fried over high heat at a temperature of 350°F. (180°C.). Batter-coated ingredients are fried at a lower temperature of 250°F.–300°F. (120°C.–150°C.). You may want to use a deep-frying thermometer. When the proper temperature has been reached, add ingredients one at a time, frying a small amount at a time, so a constant temperature can be maintained. Ingredients should be stirred or turned to ensure even browning.

Seasonings and Cornstarch Coating Before Deep-Frying

All ingredients should be cut into pieces of approximately the same size. Remove any moisture with paper towels. Some recipes do not require seasoning before frying, but many call for a marinade of Chinese rice wine or sake, soy sauce, salt and pepper. The marinating time may vary from 5 minutes to 1 hour, depending on the size of the ingredients and the amounts of seasonings. After marinating, egg and cornstarch are kneaded into ingredients. If any excess water collects in the bottom of the bowl, drain it out and add more cornstarch. It is best to have a light egg-cornstarch batter. If too much cornstarch has been added and the ingredients stick together, thin batter by adding a small amount of wine or sake and oil. This coating serves to preserve moisture, flavor and nutrients.

Stir-Frying

Stir-frying is a very common Chinese cooking method, where ingredients are fried in a small amount of oil over high heat for a very short time. All preparations such as washing, chopping, marinating, parboiling and deep-frying should be completed prior to stir-frying.

Heat wok over low heat for about 1 minute. Add 2–3 tablespoons oil and heat over high heat for 5–30 seconds. Add ingredients and stir and toss for a short time. When done, the food should still be crisp and firm. Serve immediately.

Steaming

Steaming allows food to be heated thoroughly without loss of juices or change in color.

Bring water in wok to a boil. Place steamer in wok, cover and heat. The water should almost touch the bottom of the steamer.

Food may be placed directly on steamer or in a dish on the steamer. Cover. Reduce heat to maintain a gentle boil. Steam.

Avoid lifting the cover so steam does not escape. Remove food immediately when done to avoid overcooking in hot steamer.

It may be necessary to add boiling water during cooking to maintain water level.

Stewing and Simmering

Stewing is a method of simmering foods in a liquid base over low heat for a long time. Meats may be browned before stewing. Commonly, the pot is covered with a lid to preserve juices. Sometimes, the lid is not used, allowing the liquid to evaporate.

Thickening

Cornstarch is added to sauces and soups to thicken. It is often dissolved in cold water and mixed thoroughly to make a smooth paste. Add paste slowly to heating dish, stirring constantly until smooth and thick.

Sauces

Sauces may dress meats, fish or vegetable dishes. Sauces may be poured over hot food immediately after cooking, or when cooled. Other sauces are served at the table as a dip.

Soup

Since the Chinese traditionally serve soup last or between courses, the other dishes to be served must be considered when choosing a soup. Soups may be elegant and clear or hearty and thick with pieces of meats, fish and vegetables. Soup stock, often flavored with chicken, green onion and ginger, is a common ingredient in many recipes.

Cutting and Slicing

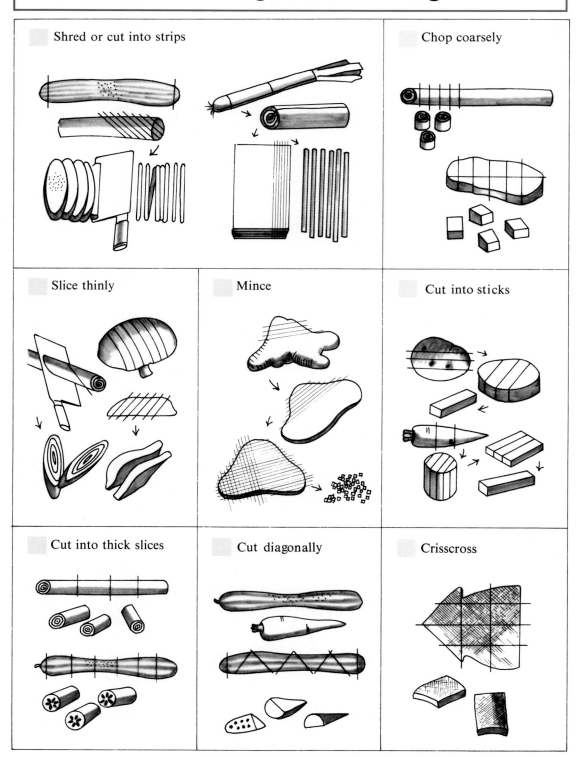

Shred or cut into strips

Chop coarsely

Slice thinly

Mince

Cut into sticks

Cut into thick slices

Cut diagonally

Crisscross

Basic Methods

Stir-Fried Beef with Broccoli

4 servings
Ingredients:
⅔ lb. (300 g) beef fillet, in ⅛-inch (3 mm) slices
Seasonings:
   1½ teaspoons cornstarch
   1½ teaspoons Chinese rice wine or sake
   1½ teaspoons soy sauce
   1½ teaspoons vegetable oil
   dash of pepper
11 oz. (300 g) fresh broccoli
½ green onion
1 fresh ginger
2½–3 cups vegetable oil for frying meat
3 tablespoons vegetable oil for stir-frying vegetables
½ teaspoon salt
2 tablespoons Chinese rice wine or sake
1 teaspoon sesame oil
pepper

Method:
1. Cut off and discard large leaves and tough end of broccoli stalks. Split stalks almost up to flowerets to ensure even cooking. Parboil broccoli in lightly salted boiling water for 1 minute. Drain. **(1)**
2. Cut green onion diagonally into ¼-inch (5 mm) slices. Peel skin from ginger; cut into thin slices.
3. Cut beef slices into 1½-inch (4–5 cm) squares. Combine seasonings; stir until thickened. Add beef and stir to coat evenly. **(2–3)**
4. Heat 2½–3 cups vegetable oil in wok over medium-low heat. Add beef and deep-fry for 1–2 minutes; beef should still be slightly pink. Remove beef. Drain oil from wok. **(4)**
5. Heat 3 tablespoons vegetable oil in wok over high heat. Stir-fry green onions and ginger for 10 seconds. Add broccoli, salt, wine and beef. Sprinkle with pepper and sesame oil. Stir-fry until thoroughly heated, for 10 seconds. **(5–6)**

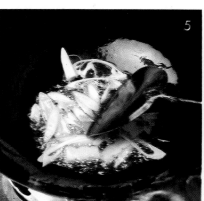

15

Stir-Fried Pork with Chinese Pickles

4 servings
Ingredients:
5 oz. (150 g) pork ham, cut into ¼-inch (5 mm) slices
3½ oz. (100 g) fresh bamboo shoots, boiled
1–2 Chinese pickles (*cha-ts'ai*)
Seasonings:
   1 teaspoon cornstarch
   2 teaspoons Chinese rice wine or sake
   1 teaspoon soy sauce
2 cups vegetable oil for frying meat
2 tablespoons vegetable oil for stir-frying vegetables
1 tablespoon Chinese rice wine or sake
1½ teaspoons soy sauce
1 teaspoon sesame oil

Method:
1.   Remove and discard red pepper from Chinese pickles. Cut pickles into thin strips. Rinse with water to remove salt. **(1)**
2.   Cut pork into 1½-inch (4–5 cm) lengths. Cut bamboo shoots into thin strips.
3.   Combine seasonings in bowl; stir until thickened. Add pork and stir to coat evenly. **(2)**
4.   Heat 2 cups vegetable oil in wok over medium-low heat. Add pork and deep-fry for 10 seconds, until meat is white. Remove pork. Drain oil from wok. **(3–4)**
5.   Heat 2 tablespoons vegetable oil in wok over high heat. Add bamboo shoots; stir-fry for 15 seconds. Add Chinese pickles, wine, soy sauce and pork. Stir-fry to heat through. Sprinkle with sesame oil. **(5–6)**

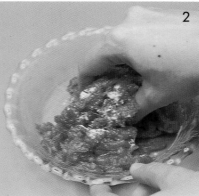

Stir-Fried Beef with Oyster Sauce

4 servings

Ingredients:

⅔ lb. (300 g) beef fillet, cut into ⅕-inch (5 mm)
   slices

Marinade:
   1 tablespoon Chinese rice wine or sake
   1 tablespoon soy sauce
   1½ teaspoons cornstarch
   1½ teaspoons vegetable oil
   dash of pepper

Seasonings:
   ⅔ cup chicken soup stock (see page 95)
   ¼ teaspoon salt

1 teaspoon Chinese rice wine or sake
1 teaspoon cornstarch, dissolved in
   1 tablespoon cold water
1 teaspoon sesame oil
2 cups vegetable oil for frying meat
2 tablespoons vegetable oil for stir-frying
   vegetables
½ head lettuce, washed, drained and
   separated
1 tablespoon oyster sauce
pepper

Method:

1. Cut beef into bite-size pieces, 1½-inch (4–5 cm) squares. Combine marinade ingredients.
   Add beef and mix well.
2. Combine soup stock, salt, wine, cornstarch and sesame oil. Set aside.
3. Heat 2 cups vegetable oil in wok over high heat. Deep-fry beef mixture for 1–2 minutes. Remove beef.
4. Heat 2 tablespoons vegetable oil in wok over high heat. Stir-fry lettuce for 3–4 seconds. Add
   seasonings and beef. Stir-fry to heat thoroughly. Season with oyster sauce and pepper.

Stir-Fried Beef with Tomato

4 servings

Ingredients:

⅔ lb. (300 g) beef fillet,
   cut into ⅕-inch (5 mm) slices
Seasonings:
   1½ teaspoons Chinese rice wine or sake
   2 teaspoons soy sauce
   2 teaspoons cornstarch
   dash of pepper
2 cups vegetable oil for frying meat
1 large tomato
1 clove garlic, minced

2 tablespoons vegetable oil
½ cup beef soup stock
1 tablespoon Chinese rice wine or sake
1 teaspoon soy sauce
½ teaspoon salt
1 teaspoon sugar, if desired
1 teaspoon cornstarch,
   dissolved in 3 teaspoons water
sesame oil

Method:

1. Cut beef into bite-size pieces, about 1½-inch (4–5 cm) squares. Combine seasoning ingredients in a bowl. Add beef and mix well. Deep-fry over medium-low heat for 2 minutes, until meat is brown.
2. Immerse tomato in boiling water for 30 seconds, and then in cold water. Peel skin off. Cut into thick slices and remove seeds.
3. Heat 2 tablespoons vegetable oil in wok over high heat. Stir-fry garlic for 15 seconds. Add beef, tomato slices, soup stock, wine, soy sauce, salt and sugar. Bring to a boil. Reduce heat. Stir in dissolved cornstarch until thickened, about 2–3 minutes. Sprinkle with sesame oil.

Stir-Fried Lamb with Vegetable Chunks

4 servings
Ingredients:
7 oz. (200 g) lamb, sliced
Seasonings:
   dash of pepper
   1½ tablespoons Chinese rice wine or sake
   1½ teaspoons soy sauce
   1 teaspoon cornstarch
2 hot red peppers, seeded and cut into rings
4 medium green peppers, and cut into bite-size chunks
4 dried Chinese mushrooms

4 oz. (100 g) cooked bamboo shoots
1 carrot
2 cups vegetable oil for frying meat
½ teaspoon salt
1 tablespoon Chinese rice wine or sake
1 teaspoon soy sauce
1 teaspoon sugar
½ teaspoon sesame oil

Method:
1. Cut lamb into bite-size pieces. Add seasonings and set aside.
2. Soak mushrooms in lukewarm water for 30 minutes. Squeeze to drain well. Discard stems; cut into bite-size chunks.
3. Thinly slice the bamboo shoots and carrot lengthwise; cut into bite-size chunks.
4. Heat 2 cups oil in wok over medium heat. Stir-fry lamb for 1–2 minutes, until meat is white. Remove lamb.
5. Heat 3 tablespoons vegetable oil in wok over high heat. Stir-fry vegetabels for 30 seconds. Add salt, wine, soy sauce, sugar, and lamb. Stir-fry to heat through. Sprinkle with sesame oil.

Three Mushroom Chicken

4 servings
Ingredients:

2 chicken wings
  ¼ teaspoon salt
  1 tablespoon Chinese rice wine or sake
1 teaspoon cornstarch
2 cups vegetable oil for deep-frying
5 oz. (150 g) fresh or canned straw
  mushrooms
6 fresh Chinese mushrooms

5 oz. (150 g) fresh Japanese mushrooms (*shimeji*)
2 tablespoons vegetable oil for stir-frying
½ teaspoon salt
2 tablespoons Chinese rice wine or sake
3 tablespoons soup stock (see page 95)
soy sauce
pepper
½ teaspoon sesame oil

Method:
1. Cut chicken diagonally into slices. Season with ¼ teaspoon salt and 1 tablespoon wine. Coat with cornstarch.
2. Heat 2 cups vegetable oil in wok over high heat. Coat chicken with cornstarch. Deep-fry for 1–2 minutes until meat is white. Remove chicken on paper towels.
3. Cut straw mushrooms in half. Discard stems of Chinese mushrooms and cut diagonally into slices. Discard stems of Japanese mushrooms and split into flowerets.
4. Heat 2 tablespoons vegetable oil in wok. Stir-fry straw mushrooms for 15 seconds. Add Chinese and Japanese mushrooms, salt, wine, soup, soy sauce, and chicken. Stir-fry until heated through and until mushrooms are soft. Sprinkle with pepper and sesame oil.

Stir-Fried Lamb with Pickled Mustard Greens

4 servings

Ingredients:

7 oz. (200 g) lamb, partially frozen, thinly sliced
5 oz. (150 g) pickled mustard greens
1-inch (2.5 cm) fresh ginger, cut into thin strips
3 tablespoons vegetable oil for stir-frying
1 tablespoon Chinese rice wine or sake
½ tablespoon soy sauce
½ teaspoon sugar
drop of sesame oil

Method:

1. Cut lamb, while still partially frozen for easier slicing, into thin strips about 1½ inches (4 cm) long. Cut mustard greens into thin strips 1½ inches (4 cm) long.
2. Heat 3 tablespoons vegetable oil in wok over high heat. Stir-fry ginger for 15 seconds. Add lamb and mustard greens.
3. Add wine, soy sauce, sugar and sesame oil. Stir-fry for 2 minutes.

Stir-Fried Chicken Livers

4 servings
Ingredients:
1 1b. (400 g) chicken livers
Marinade:
    ½ fresh ginger, sliced
    1 green onion, sliced
    1 tablespoon Chinese rice wine or sake
    2 tablespoons soy sauce
    salt
    pepper
    ¼ teaspoon five-spice powder (*wu-hsiang-fên*)
½ egg
1 tablespoon cornstarch

3 cups vegetable oil for deep-frying
5 medium green peppers, cut into bite-size pieces
½ onion, cut into bite-size pieces
2 tablespoons vegetable oil for stir-frying
1 green onion, sliced
½ fresh ginger, sliced
3¼ oz. (100 g) boiled bamboo shoots, sliced
⅓ teaspoon salt
pepper
1½ teaspoons Chinese rice wine or sake
½ teaspoon sesame oil

Method:
1. Wash chicken livers and cut into bite-size pieces. Combine marinade ingredients. Marinate chicken livers for ½–1 hour.
2. Put chicken livers into a bowl; add egg and cornstarch. Mix well.
3. Heat 3 cups vegetable oil in wok over low heat. Deep-fry chicken livers for 3 minutes until golden brown. Remove. Deep-fry green peppers and onion over high heat for 1 minute. Remove.
4. Heat 2 tablespoons vegetable oil in wok and stir-fry green onion and ginger until they exude fragrance, about 30 seconds. Add bamboo shoots, chicken livers, green peppers and onion. Sprinkle with salt, wine, pepper and sesame oil. Stir-fry for 10 seconds.

Stir-Fried Egg with Crabmeat

4 servings
Ingredients:
5 oz. (150 g) vegetable mixture (green onion, carrot, bean sprouts and scallions)
7 oz. (200 g) canned crabmeat, drained and boned
1 oz. (30 g) bean threads
5 eggs, beaten
7 tablespoons vegetable oil for stir-frying
salt
pepper
½ teaspoon sesame oil

Method:
1. Finely shred green onions and carrots into 1–inch (3 cm) lengths. Cut scallions into 1–inch (3 cm) lengths. Parboil bean sprouts and scallions in lightly salted water for 1 minute. Drain.
2. Flake crabmeat. Beat eggs. Salt and pepper to taste. Soak bean threads in hot water until transparent.* Drain and cut into bite-size pieces. **(1)**
3. Heat 7 tablespoons vegetable oil in wok over medium heat. First stir-fry green onion, then add carrot, and finally bean sprouts, scallions, crabmeat and bean threads. Season with salt, pepper and sesame oil. **(2–3)**
4. Pour in eggs. When the bottom of egg mixture is partially set, stir-fry until evenly golden browned. **(4)**

* As many bean threads may be used as desired. Do not soak them too long, or they won't absorb the liquid from sautéed vegetables.

Chinese-Style Beefsteak

4 servings
Ingredients:
1 lb. (500 g) beef fillet
Marinade:
   2 tablespoons Chinese rice wine or sake
   2 tablespoons soy sauce
   2 tablespoons water
   dash of pepper
1 tablespoon cornstarch
½ teaspoon salt
1 bunch spinach or *ching-kêng-ts'ai*
3 cups vegetable oil for deep-drying

Method:
1. Cut beef into slices, about ½ inch (1.5 cm) thick. Combine marinade ingredients. Add beef. Let stand for 15 minutes. Sprinkle with cornstarch and mix well. **(1–2)**
2. Place spinach in lightly salted boiling water. Cover and bring to a boil. Reduce heat and simmer for 1 minute, until soft. Drain. Keep warm. **(3)**
3. Heat 3 cups vegetable oil in wok to 320°F. (160°C.). Add beef, piece by piece. Deep-fry for 2–3 minutes. Do not overcook. **(4)**
4. Place beef on serving platter. Place drained spinach around the beef. Serve with rice.

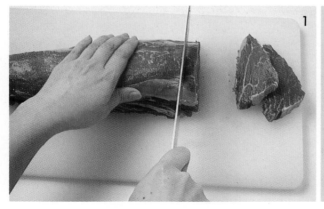

3

4

Sweet and Sour Pork

4 servings

Ingredients:

1 lb. (500 g) lean pork ham, cut into 1 × 2-inch (2.5 × 4 cm) squares

Marinade:
   1 tablespoon Chinese rice wine or sake
   1 tablespoon soy sauce
   1 egg yolk

Seasonings:
   2 tablespoons sugar
   2 tablespoons Chinese rice wine or sake
   2 tablespoons soy sauce
   2 tablespoons vinegar
   3 tablespoons ketchup
   6 tablespoons water
   1 teaspoon cornstarch
   $\frac{1}{3}$ teaspoon salt

1 carrot

2–3 medium green peppers

1 onion

1 cup canned pineapple chunks, drained

5 cups vegetable oil for deep-frying

cornstarch for coating

Method:

1. Combine marinade ingredients. Marinate pork for 20 minutes.
2. Combine seasonings and set aside.
3. Cut peeled carrot, seeded pepper and skinned onion into bite-size chunks. **(1)**
4. Heat 5 cups vegetable oil in wok over high heat. Stir-fry vegetables for 4 seconds. Remove. **(2)**
5. Reduce to medium heat. Lightly coat pork squares with cornstarch. Deep-fry for 1–2 minutes, turning occasionally, until golden brown and crisp. Remove. **(3–4)**
6. Drain oil from wok. Put on medium heat. Pour seasonings mixture into wok. Stir until thickened. Add pork, vegetables and pineapple. Stir-fry until heated through. **(5–6)**

4

5

6

Tempura

4 servings

Ingredients:
8 prawns, about 4 inches (10 cm) long
8 small green peppers
4–5 stalks green asparagus
1 medium-sized sweet potato
Batter:
   1 egg
   cold water
   1 cup flour, sifted
5 cups vegetable oil for deep-frying
Tentsuyu sauce:
   1 cup bonito (or chicken) soup stock, cold
   ¼ cup soy sauce
   ¼ cup *mirin*
grated giant white raddish

Method:
1. Shell and devein prawns, leaving tails on. So prawns will not curl when fried, make a few cuts on inside curve. Cut off tips of tails. **(1–2)**
2. Make ½-inch (12 mm) lengthwise cuts in the center of each pepper so it will stand when fried. Cut sweet potato into ⅓-inch (8 mm) thick slices, soak in water for 30 minutes and pat dry with paper towel. Remove tough stem end from asparagus and parboil in lightly salted water for 3 minutes, until it is almost tender. Soak in cold water for 1 minute and drain.
3. Break egg into measuring cup and add cold water to the level of 1 cup. Pour into bowl, add flour and mix lightly. **(3)**
4. Heat 5 cups vegetable oil in wok to 360°F. (180°C.). Lightly coat prawns with flour and dip into batter. Deep-fry for 2 minutes, until crisp. **(4–5)**
5. Add a little extra flour to the batter to thicken. Lightly coat vegetables with flour and dip into batter. Deep-fry for 2 minutes, until crisp.

Notes:
* Heat a generous quantity of oil in deep pan.
* Try to keep oil temperature at 350°–360°F. by adding ingredients gradually.
* Fry a small amount at a time.
* Make the batter a little thicker for vegetables than for shellfish because vegetables contain more water.

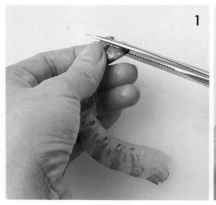
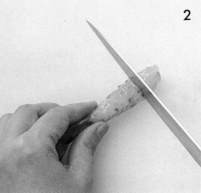

Deep-Fried Chicken in Potato Coats

4 servings

Ingredients:

2 chicken thighs
  1 tablespoon Chinese rice wine or sake
  ⅓ teaspoon salt
Potato coating:
  11 oz. (300 g) potatoes
  3 fresh Chinese mushrooms
  ½ green onion, minced
  ½ teaspoon salt
  dash of pepper
  1 egg yolk
2 tablespoons vegetable oil for stir-frying
3 cups vegetable oil for frying
cornstarch for coating
flour for coating

Batter:
  ⅓ cup flour
  ⅓ cup cornstarch
  ⅓ cup water
  1 egg yolk
4 lettuce leaves
Shredded vegetable garnish:
  ¼ cup shredded giant white radish
  ¼ cup shredded carrot
  ¼ cup shredded cucumber
Vinegar sauce:
  1 tablespoon soy sauce
  1 tablespoon sugar
  1½ tablespoons vinegar
  1 teaspoon sesame oil

Method:

1. Sprinkle chicken with wine and salt. Place in steamer. Steam for 10 minutes. Let cool. Bone and slice chicken. **(1)**
2. Peel potatoes. Place in lightly salted boiling water. Cover and bring to a boil. Reduce heat and simmer for 20 minutes. Drain. Mash potatoes well.
3. Discard mushroom stems and mince.
4. Heat 2 tablespoons vegetable oil in wok over high heat. Stir-fry mushrooms and green onion for 15 seconds. Remove.
5. Combine all ingredients for potato coating.
6. Dry chicken on paper towels. Lightly coat with cornstarch. Evenly spread potato coating on chicken. Lightly coat with flour. Preheat 3 cups vegetable oil in wok to 340°F. (170°C.). **(2–3)**
7. Combine batter ingredients. Dip chicken in batter. Fry for 2–3 minutes, turning occasionally, until golden brown and crisp. Drain on paper towels.
8. Slice chicken into bite-size pieces. Arrange on serving platter. Garnish with shredded vegetables on lettuce leaves, sprinkled with vinegar sauce.

Deep-Fried Meatballs

4 servings

Ingredients:

1 lb. (400 g) ground pork

3–4 dried Chinese mushrooms

1 green onion, minced

1 egg

Seasonings:

   1 tablespoon cornstarch

   1 tablespoon Chinese rice wine or sake

   1 teaspoon vegetable oil

   ½ teaspoon salt

   ⅛ teaspoon five-spice powder (*wu-hsiang-fên*)

   dash of pepper

   ½ teaspoon sesame oil

5–6 cups vegetable oil for deep-frying

few sprigs of parsley

Method:

1. Soak mushrooms in cold water for 1 hour. Squeeze to drain well. Discard stems; chop mushrooms. **(1)**
2. Combine pork, mushrooms, onion, egg and seasonings. Knead well. **(2)**
3. Shape into 1-inch (3 cm) balls. **(3–4)**
4. Heat 5–6 cups vegetable oil in wok to 330°F. (165°C). Add meatballs. Stir occasionally until evenly browned and thoroughly cooked. Remove and drain on paper towels.
5. Arrange meatballs on serving platter; garnish with parsley.

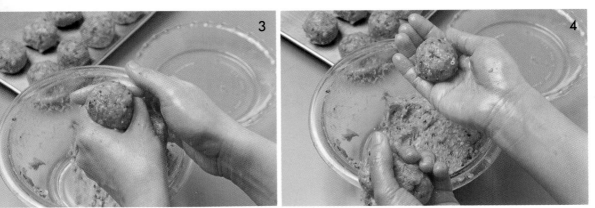

3

4

Fried Eggplant with Shrimp

4 servings

Ingredients:

4–5 medium-sized eggplants, about 2 inches (5 cm) in diameter
7 oz. (200 g) shrimp
4 oz. (80–100 g) pork fat, minced
½ teaspoon salt
1–2 teaspoons Chinese rice wine or sake
1 teaspoon ginger juice
½ egg white
1 tablespoon cornstarch
cornstarch for dusting coating
4½–5 cups vegetable oil for deep-frying
sweet pickled cucumber or dill pickles for garnish

Method:

1. Cut eggplants into ½-inch (1 cm) slices. Remove excess moisture with paper towels.
2. Remove black veins from shrimp; mince.
3. Combine shrimp, pork fat, salt, wine, and ginger juice. Add egg white and cornstarch. Knead well. **(1)**
4. Dip one side of each eggplant slice into cornstarch to help the shrimp mixture cling to the eggplant. **(2)**
5. Place a small amount of the shrimp mixture on the cornstarch-coated side of the eggplant. Smooth the shrimp with a knife to form a mound about ½-inch (1 cm) high. **(3)**
6. Heat 4½–5 cups vegetable oil in wok to 350°F. (175°C.). Reduce heat to low. Place eggplant slices, with the shrimp side up, in oil. Fry for 2 minutes, turning often, until golden brown. **(4)**
7. Serve hot. Garnish with sweet pickled cucumber or dill pickles.

3

4

Sansho Shrimp

4 servings
Ingredients:

8–10 jumbo shrimp (about 1 lb., 500 g)
Marinade:
   3–4 thin slices of ginger
   ½ green onion, thinly sliced
   1 tablespoon Chinese rice wine or sake
   ⅓ teaspoon salt
3 tablespoons flour

5 cups vegetable oil for deep-frying
Sansho pepper-salt:
   ½ teaspoon salt
   ½ teaspoon pepper
   ½ teaspoon powdered *sansho*
1 tablespoon chopped parsley

Method:

1. Remove legs from shrimp. Slit the tail. Make a shallow cut lengthwise down the back of each shrimp. Remove black vein.
2. Combine marinade ingredients. Add shrimp. Let stand for 30 minutes, turning shrimp occasionally. Remove shrimp; dry on paper towels. Coat with flour; shake gently to remove excess flour.
3. Heat 5 cups vegetable oil in wok to 360°F. (182°C.). Add shrimp and deep-fry for 2 minutes.
4. Remove shrimp to serving platter. Combine ingredients for *sansho* pepper-salt and sprinkle on shrimp. Sprinkle with chopped parsley.

Crispy Chicken with Ginger-Garlic Sauce

4 servings

Ingredients:

2 chicken thighs

Marinade:
    1 tablespoon Chinese rice wine or sake
    1 tablespoon soy sauce

Sauce:
    1 tablespoon minced green onion
    1 tablespoon minced fresh ginger
    1 tablespoon minced garlic

2–3 tablespoons soy sauce
2 tablespoons sugar
1 tablespoon vinegar
1 teaspoon sesame oil
few drops of hot pepper oil
cornstarch for coating
5 cups vegetable oil for deep-frying

Method:

1. Cut chicken thighs in half horizontally. Combine marinade ingredients. Marinate chicken for 1 hour.
2. Combine sauce ingredients. Set aside.
3. Dry chicken on paper towels. Lightly coat with cornstarch.
4. Heat 5 cups vegetable oil in wok over high heat. Deep-fry chicken for 3–5 minutes, until golden brown. Remove chicken. Drain oil from wok. Slice chicken into ½-inch (1 cm) slices. Re-assemble slices on serving platter.
5. Pour sauce mixture over chicken.

Stewed Chinese Cabbage with Scallops

4 servings

Ingredients:

3–4 large dried scallops

6–7 Chinese cabbage leaves

2–3 tablespoons vegetable oil for frying scallops

1 tablespoon Chinese rice wine or sake

1½–2 cups chicken soup stock and reserved scallop water

½ teaspoon salt

2 teaspoons cornstarch, dissolved in 6 teaspoons cold water

1 teaspoon ginger juice

Method:

1. Rinse scallops. Cover with hot water. Cover and let stand overnight or 8 hours. Drain water and reserve. Flake scallops into small pieces. **(1)**
2. Place cabbage leaves in just enough lightly salted boiling water to cover. Parboil for 2 minutes, or until tender; drain. Cut into ½ × 4-inch (1 × 10 cm) strips. **(2)**
3. Heat 2–3 tablespoons oil in wok over high heat. Drain any excess water from scallops. Stir-fry scallops for 1 minute. **(3)**
4. Add wine, soup stock and reserved scallop water to wok. Bring to a boil; add Chinese cabbage and salt. Cover; reduce heat and simmer for 5–7 minutes, until cabbage is tender. **(3)**
5. Slowly add cornstarch mixture to soup mixture, stirring until thickened. Sprinkle with ginger juice. **(5)**

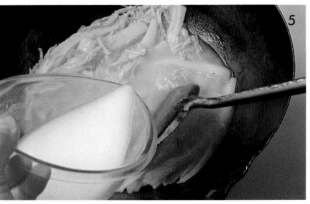

Braised Pork

4 servings
Ingredients:
1¾ lb. (750 g) pork (bacon slub)
3 cups vegetable oil for deep-frying
½ green onion
1 fresh ginger
2 star anise
Seasonings:
   1 tablespoon sugar
   2 tablespoons Chinese rice wine or sake
   ⅓ cup soy sauce, divided in half
1 bunch of *ching-kêng-ts'ai* or mustard greens
salt
½ teaspoons vegetable oil
1 teaspoon cornstarch, dissolved in 1 tablespoon cold water

Method:
1. Cut pork in half lengthwise. Heat 3 cups vegetable oil in wok over high heat. Deep-fry pork for 3 minutes, until lightly brown. Remove pork. **(1)**
2. Crush green onion and fresh ginger lightly with the blunt edge of knife to release flavor.
3. Place pork in cooking pot. Season with sugar, wine, and half of the soy sauce. Add cold water just to cover. Add green onion, ginger and star anise. Cover and bring to a boil. Reduce heat and simmer for 1 hour. Add remaining half of soy sauce. **(2)**
4. Remove pork and let cool. Cut into ½-inch (1 cm) slices. Line the bottom of a bowl with pork slices, fat side down. Top with green onion, ginger and star anise. Add cooked liquid from pot. **(3–4)**
5. Fill wok ⅘ full of hot water. Place steamer in wok and preheat over medium heat. Place bowl in steamer and steam for 1 hour.
6. Wash *ching-kêng-ts'ai*. Place in lightly salted boiling water. Add ½ teaspoon vegetable oil. Cover and bring to a boil. Reduce heat and simmer for 3 minutes. Drain.
7. Drain cooking liquid from pork into a saucepan. Discard green onion, ginger and star anise. Place pork on serving platter. Arrange drained *ching-kên-ts'ai* around pork. **(5)**
8. Heat cooking liquid over medium heat. Add cornstarch mixture, stirring until thickened. Pour over pork. **(6)**

4

5

6

Steamed Chicken

4 servings
Ingredients:
3 chicken thighs, with bones
⅓ teaspoon salt
Sauce:
   ¼ cup soy sauce
   2 tablespoons vinegar
   2 tablespoons sugar
   2 tablespoons sesame oil
1 green onion
2 fresh ginger roots, sliced
3–4 tablespoons Chinese rice wine or sake
1 tablespoon vegetable oil
1 cucumber, thinly-sliced

Method:
1. Rinse chicken with water. Pat dry with paper towels. Rub with salt. Let stand at room temperature for 2 hours. **(1)**
2. Combine sauce ingredients; set aside.
3. Cut green onion diagonally into ⅕-inch (5 mm) thick slices. Cut ginger into ⅛-inch (3 mm) slices. Sprinkle chicken with wine. Spread onion and ginger over chicken. Set aside for 1 hour. **(2)**
4. Sprinkle chicken and vegetables with vegetable oil. Place in steamer over medium heat. Steam for 20–25 minutes. **(3)**
5. Remove chicken and vegetables. When partially cooled, cover with plastic wrap. Let cool completely. Cut each thigh into ¾-inch (2 cm) slices; reassemble thigh. **(4)**
6. Arrange cucumber slices around edges of serving platter. Place chicken pieces, skin side up, in the center. Serve with sauce.

3

4

Steamed Egg Custard with Meat Sauce

4 servings

Ingredients:

2–3 dried Chinese mushrooms and ⅓ cup mushroom liquid

2 tablespoons vegetable oil

½ green onion, minced

10 oz. (100 g) ground pork

Seasonings:

    1 tablespoon Chinese rice wine or sake

    2 tablespoons soy sauce

    ½ teaspoon sesame oil

    dash of five-spice powder

    ½ teaspoon sugar

Egg mixture:

    4 cups chicken soup stock (see page 95)

    ½ teaspoon salt

    4 eggs

1 small green pepper, minced

Method:

1. Soak Chinese mushrooms in warm water for 30 minutes. Squeeze to drain well, reserving ⅓ cup liquid. Discard stems; mince mushrooms.
2. Heat 2 tablespoons vegetable oil in wok over high heat. Stir-fry green onion, Chinese mushrooms and ground pork. When pork is whitish, add remaining seasonings. Cook 5–6 minutes. Set aside.
3. Heat soup stock to about 160°F. (70°C.) and add salt. Gradually stir soup into lightly beaten eggs. Press egg mixture through a sieve to ensure a smooth custard.   **(1)**
4. Pour egg mixture into a lightly greased bowl. Steam in hot steamer for 10–20 minutes over low heat. Place meat sauce on top of egg custard and steam for 2–3 more minutes.   **(2–4)**
5. Garnish egg custard with minced green peppers.

Pork with Garlic Sauce

4 servings
Ingredients:

1 lb. (450 g) pork (bacon slub)   Garlic sauce:
½ green onion   4 cloves garlic, grated
1 fresh ginger   ¼ cup soy sauce
¼ teaspoon salt
1 cucumber

Method:

1. Place pork in enough boiling water to cover. Remove from heat. Let stand until meat is white. Drain.
2. Cut green onion and ginger and lightly crush with the blunt edge of knife.
3. Add green onion, ginger and salt. Add cold water to cover and bring to a boil. Skim off. Reduce heat and simmer for 1 hour. Cool.
4. Slice cucumber lengthwise into very thin strips. Rinse, drain and set aside.
5. Combine ingredients for sauce and set aside.
6. Cut cooked pork into thin slices, then into ⅕ × 2 inch- (5 mm × 5 cm) squares. Arrange on serving platter. Garnish with cucumber slices.
7. The garlic sauce may be poured over the pork or served as a dip.

Steamed Pork Loaf with Salmon

4 servings

Ingredients:

Pork loaf:

15 oz. (400 g) ground pork
1 green onion, minced
1 egg
1 tablespoon cornstarch
1 tablespoon Chinese rice wine or sake

1 tablespoon ginger juice
¾ teaspoon salt
1½ teaspoons sesame oil
2–3 fillets salted salmon
4 green vegetables (mustard greens or
  ching-kêng-ts'ai)

Method:

1. Combine pork loaf ingredients and knead well.
2. Skin and bone the salmon. Cut into ½-inch (1.5 cm) squares.
3. Lightly oil a plate that will fit into steamer. Arrange salmon pieces close together in a rectangular shape on plate in single layer. Spoon pork loaf mixture on top of salmon; form into loaf shape.
4. Preheat steamer over medium heat. Place plate in steamer. Steam for 15–20 minutes.
5. Wash green vegetables. Place in lightly salted boiling water. Add a few drops of vegetable oil. Cover and bring to a boil. Reduce heat and simmer for 1 minute.
6. Take plate out of steamer. Invert over serving platter. Garnish with drained green vegetables.

Smoked Chicken

6–8 servings
Ingredients:
1 whole chicken
Stuffing:
   1 green onion, sliced
   4 sliced fresh ginger
   2 teaspoons salt
   4 tablespoons Chinese rice wine or sake
2 teaspoons sesame oil for basting
Seasonings:
   1 cup black tea leaves
   1 cup sugar
   ½ cup rice
   2 star anise, crushed
   3 bay leaves
prepared mustard soy sauce

Method:
1. Rinse chicken with water. Combine stuffing ingredients. Fill cavity with ½ of stuffing. Rub outside of chicken with remaining ½ of stuffing. Set aside for 1–1½ hours. **(1)**
2. Place chicken on plate in steamer. Steam for 1 hour. **(2)**
3. Pat chicken dry with paper towels. Remove stuffing. Rub chicken with salt. Baste with sesame oil.
4. Line bottom of wok with aluminum foil. Place seasonings on foil. Place metal rack in wok. Put chicken on rack. **(3–4)**
5. Tape newspapers inside the lid of the wok to seal in smoke. Cover and place over medium heat. Reduce to low heat when smoke appears. Cook and smoke for 20 minutes.
6. Let chicken cool. Cut (see page 96). Serve with prepared mustard and soy sauce.

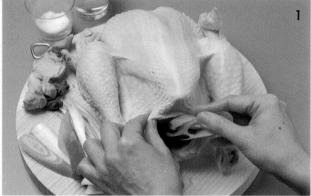

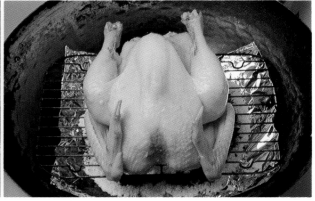

Vegetable and Bean Thread Soup

4 servings
Ingredients:
½ oz. (40 g) bean threads
3–4 cabbage leaves
1 tomato
5–6 cups soup stock (see page 95)
1 tablespoon Chinese rice wine or sake
⅔ teaspoon salt
dash of pepper

Method:
1. Cover bean threads with lukewarm water; let stand for 10 minutes. Squeeze to drain well. Cut into 3-inch (8 cm) lengths. **(1)**
2. Cut cabbage into 1-inch (3–4 cm) squares.
3. Immerse tomato in boiling water for 30 seconds, and then in cold water. Peel skin off. Cut into thin slices and remove seeds. **(2)**
4. Bring soup stock to a boil. Add cabbage and tomato. Skim. **(3)**
5. Reduce heat and simmer for 2–5 minutes, until cabbage is tender. Add wine, salt and pepper. Add bean threads and continue to cook until translucent. **(4)**

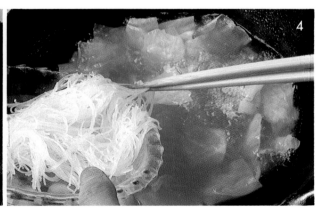

Shao-Mai

Makes 30 (4–6 servings)
Ingredients:
Filling:
   4 dried Chinese mushrooms
   10 oz. (300 g) ground pork
   1 green onion, minced
   1 egg
   1 tablespoon Chinese rice wine or sake
   1 teaspoon salt
   dash of pepper
   1½ teaspoons sesame oil
   2 teaspoons cornstarch
30 shao-mai skins
canned crabmeat, drained, boned and flaked

Method:
1. Soak mushrooms in warm water for 30 minutes. Squeeze to drain well. Discard stems; chop mushrooms.
2. Combine pork, green onion, mushrooms, egg, wine, salt, pepper, sesame oil and cornstarch. **(1)**
3. Place 1 tablespoon filling on a shao-mai skin. Press the shao-mai skins up against the filling. Fold corners out to resemble flower leaves. **(2–3)**
4. Place shao-mai ¼ inch (6 mm) apart in steamer. Arrange crabmeat on top of shao-mai. Steam over high heat for 12–15 minutes. Serve with side dishes of mustard sauce and soy sauce.

Variations:
   Green peas may be added in addition to the crab in step 3. Up to half of the pork can be substituted by flaked crabmeat or minced shrimp.

2

3

Dinner Menu

Recipes on pages 66–71

Stewed Sparerib Soup
Beef in Oyster Sauce
Sweet and Sour Pork
  with Cashews
Shrimp and Green Asparagus
  Salad
Noodles in Thick Sauce

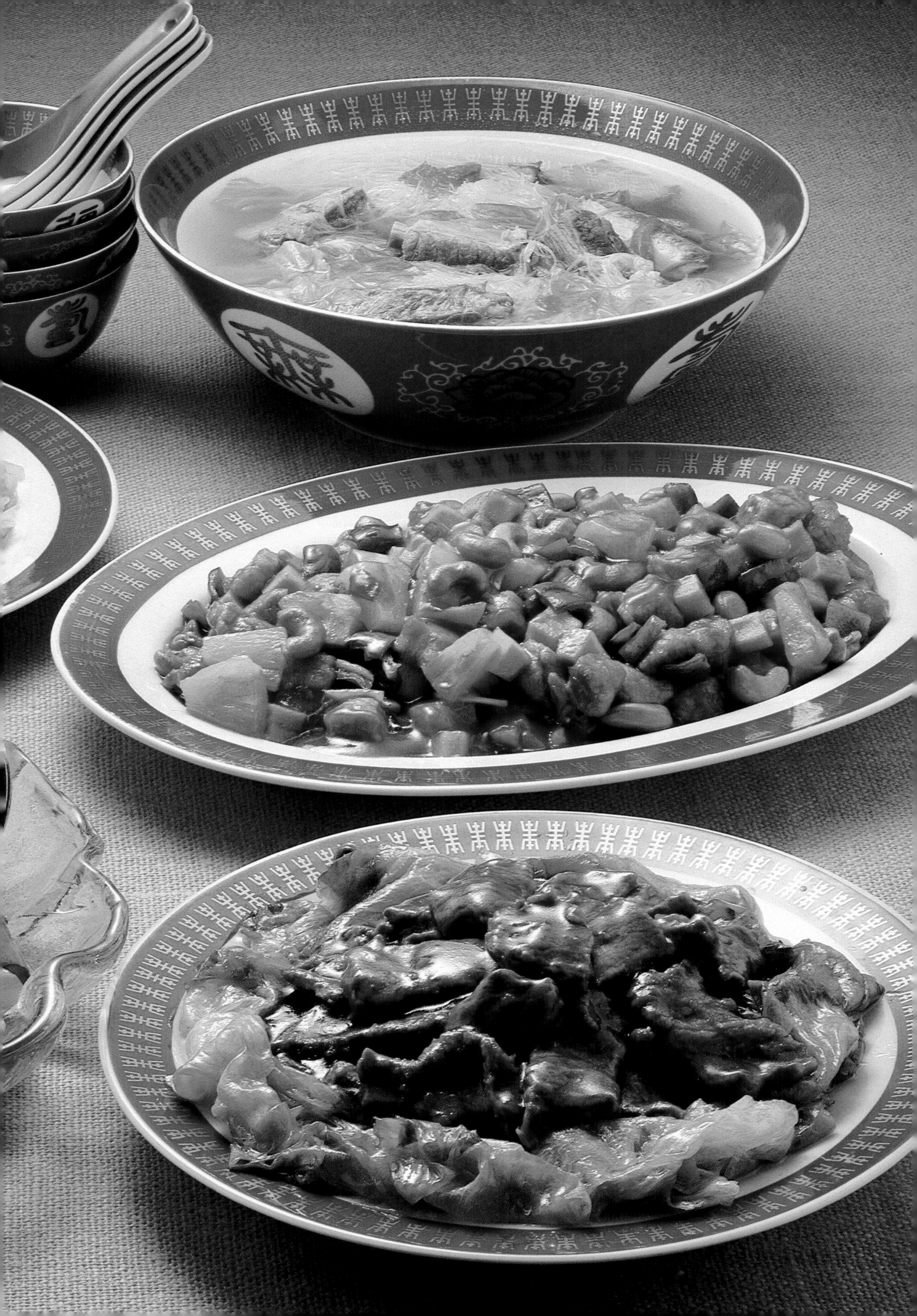

Liu (Thickening) Recipes

Recipes on pages 72–76

Scallops with White Radish
Abalone with Lettuce
Crab with Cabbage
Creamed Chicken with Corn
   and Carrots
Cuttlefish with Celery

Menu for Health

Recipes on pages 77–78

Egg and Vegetable Soup
**Sautéed Pork with String
   Beans**
Scallops and Cucumber Salad
Fried Rice with Vegetables

Snacks

Recipes on pages 81–85

Pearl Balls
Shao-mai
Pumpkin Dessert
Fried Shrimp Balls
Spring Rolls

Desserts
Recipes on pages 86–87

Almond Jelly
Sesame Custard Cakes

Dinner Menu

Pictured on pages 56–57

Stewed Sparerib Soup
Beef in Oyster Sauce
Sweet and Sour Pork with Cashews
Shrimp and Green Asparagus Salad
Noodles in Thick Sauce

Stewed Sparerib Soup

4 servings
Ingredients:
1⅛ lb. (500 g) spareribs
8 cups cold water
1 ripe tomato
1 oz. (30 g) dried bean threads
⅔ teaspoon salt

1 tablespoon Chinese rice wine or sake
2 cabbage leaves, cut into bite-size pieces
pepper
½ teaspoon sesame oil
1 teaspoon minced Chinese parsley for garnish

Method:
1. Cut spareribs into 2-inch (5 cm) lengths and wash thoroughly. Cook spareribs in boiling water until meat turns white, about 3 minutes; drain. Place spareribs in wok,

add 8 cups cold water and bring to a boil. Skim thoroughly and reduce heat. Simmer 30 minutes.

2. Immerse tomato in boiling water for 30 seconds, and then in cold water. Peel skin. Cut into slices and remove seeds. Soak bean threads in hot water until transparent. Drain and cut into bite-size pieces.

3. Add salt and wine to the soup. Add cabbage, tomato and skim thoroughly. Add bean threads. Season with pepper and sesame oil. Sprinkle with Chinese parsley.

Beef in Oyster Sauce

4 servings

Ingredients:

2/3 lb. (300 g) beef, cut into 1/5-inch (5 mm) slices

Marinade:

  2 teaspoons Chinese rice wine or sake

  2 teaspoons soy sauce

  dash of pepper

  2 teaspoons cornstarch

3 cups vegetable oil for deep-frying

1/2 head lettuce, washed, drained and separated

Seasonings:

  1/2 cup soup stock (see page 95)

  1 tablespoon Chinese rice wine or sake

  1 tablespoon oyster sauce

  dash of pepper

  1/2 teaspoon salt

  1/2 teaspoon sesame oil

  1 teaspoon cornstarch

Method:

1. Cut sliced beef into 1/4-inch (5 mm) squares. Combine marinade ingredients. Add beef and stir to coat evenly. Heat 3 cups vegetable oil in wok over medium heat. Deep-fry beef for 1 minute, until meat changes color. Remove.

2. Place lettuce in lightly salted and oiled boiling water for 30 seconds. Drain and place on serving plate.

3. Combine seasonings in wok. Bring to a boil, add beef and stir. Quickly spoon onto lettuce. Serve immediately, or lettuce will become soggy and discolored.

Sweet and Sour Pork with Cashews

4 servings

Ingredients:

½ lb. (200 g) sweet potatoes
½ lb. (200 g) pork fillet
salt
pepper
1 tablespoon Chinese rice wine or sake
1 teaspoon cornstarch
2 oz. (70 g) cashew nuts
2 medium green peppers, cut into ½-inch
  (1 cm) cubes
4 pineapple slices, cut into ½-inch (1 cm) cubes
½ green onion, chopped, about ½-inch (1 cm)
  lengths
1 clove of garlic, thinly sliced
4 slices of fresh ginger
3 cups vegetable oil for deep-frying
2 tablespoons vegetable oil
1 teaspoon *tou-pan-chiang* (hot brown bean
  paste)
Seasonings:
  ⅓ cup soup stock (see page 95)
  1 tablespoon soy sauce
  ½ teaspoon salt
  2 tablespoons ketchup
  1 teaspoon sugar

1 tablespoon Chinese rice wine or sake
½ teaspoon vinegar
1 teaspoon sesame oil
1 teaspoon cornstarch

Method:

1. Cut sweet potatoes into ½-inch (1 cm) cubes. Soak in cold water for 30 minutes, changing water occasionally. Drain and pat dry with paper towels.

2. Cut pork fillet into ½-inch (1 cm) cubes. Sprinkle with salt, pepper and wine. Let stand 5–10 minutes.

3. Lightly coat pork with cornstarch. Heat 3 cups vegetable oil over medium heat in wok. Deep-fry pork for 3 minutes, until golden brown. Remove. Deep-fry sweet potato over medium heat, until lightly brown. Remove. Deep-fry green peppers over high heat for 1 minute. Remove.

4. Deep-fry cashew nuts over low heat until lightly brown. Remove. Drain oil from wok.

5. Combine seasonings in bowl.

6. Heat 2 tablespoons vegetable oil in wok and stir-fry green onion, garlic and ginger until fragrant. Add hot brown bean paste and seasonings and bring to a boil. Add pork, sweet potato, cashew nuts, pineapples and green peppers. Heat thoroughly.

Shrimp and Green Asparagus Salad

4 servings

Ingredients:

7 oz. (200 g) small shrimp
½ teaspoon salt
2–3 tablespoons Chinese rice wine or sake
10 stalks green asparagus
½ stalk celery
1 medium green pepper
½ carrot
Dressing:
  juice of ½ lemon
  ⅔ teaspoon salt
  2 teaspoons sugar
  1 teaspoon sesame oil
  1 teaspoon oil

Method:

1. Devein shrimp. Place shrimp in wok and sprinkle with salt and wine. Cover and boil until shrimp become red, stirring occasionally to cook evenly. Let cool in wok. Shell.
2. Remove tough stem ends from asparagus. Boil asparagus in lightly salted boiling water for 5 minutes, until soft. Drain. Cut into 1½-inch (4 cm) lengths.
3. Cut celery, green peppers and carrot into thin strips. Place in cold water for 5 minutes. Drain.
4. Combine shrimp and Dressing. Add the celery, green peppers, carrot and asparagus. Chill. Place on serving bowl.

Noodles in Thick Sauce

4 servings
Ingredients:
3 packages dried Chinese noodles
1 tablespoon vegetable oil
½ green onion, minced
¼ cup dried shrimp
3–4 dried Chinese mushrooms
7 oz. (200 g) pork
1 tablespoon Chinese rice wine or sake
1 tablespoon soy sauce
pepper
½ carrot
5 oz. (150 g) giant white raddish
3½ oz. (100 g) bamboo shoots, boiled and
   drained
salt
3 tablespoons vegetable oil for stir-frying
5 cups soup stock, reserved shrimp water and
   mushroom water
2 teaspoons salt

1 teaspoon soy sauce
2 tablespoons Chinese rice wine or sake
3 eggs
1 tablespoon cornstarch, dissolved in
  3 tablespoons cold water
pepper
½ teaspoon sesame oil
2 teaspoons minced green onions for garnish

Method:
1. Place Chinese noodles in boiling water. Boil for 1–5 minutes, until tender. Drain and sprinkle with oil.
2. Soak dried shrimp in lukewarm water for 30 minutes. Drain water and reserve. Soak dried Chinese mushrooms in lukewarm water for 30 minutes. Squeeze to drain well. Reserve water. Discard stems; cut into ½-inch (1 cm) cubes. Cut bamboo shoots into ½-inch (1 cm) cubes.
3. Cut pork into ½-inch (1 cm) cubes. Sprinkle with wine, soy sauce and pepper. Set aside.
4. Pare carrot and giant white raddish, cut into ½-inch (1 cm) cubes. Place in lightly salted boiling water. Cook for 3 minutes, until crisp-tender. Drain.
5. Heat 3 tablespoons vegetable oil in wok and stir-fry green onion until fragrant. Add shrimp and stir-fry for 1 minute. Then add pork and stir-fry until meat is whitish. Add mushrooms, carrot, raddish and bamboo shoots. Season with salt, soy sauce and wine.
6. Bring soup stock to a boil in large saucepan. Add meats and vegetables. Simmer for 5 minutes, until raddish is tender.
7. Stir in dissolved cornstarch and beaten eggs. Season with pepper and sesame oil. Turn off heat. Cover pan and let stand; when eggs are half set, stir vigorously.
8. Place noodles in serving bowl, pour in thick soup. Garnish with green onions.

Liu (Thickening) Recipes

Pictured on pages 58–59

Scallops with White Radish
Abalone with Lettuce
Crab with Cabbage
Creamed Chicken with Corn and Carrots
Cuttlefish with Celery

Scallops with White Radish

4 servings

Ingredients:

5 dried scallops
1 giant white radish
2 tablespoons vegetable oil for frying
1½ cups scallop liquid plus water
½ teaspoon salt
1 tablespoon Chinese rice wine or sake
1 tablespoon cornstarch, dissolved in
  2 tablespoons cold water

Method:

1. Add hot water to scallops, just to cover. Let soak for 12 hours. Drain liquid and reserve. Flake scallops.
2. Peel white radish. Scoop out with melon baller. Place in lightly salted boiling water. Cover and bring to a boil. Reduce heat and simmer for 2 minutes, until soft. Drain.
3. Heat 2 tablespoons vegetable oil in wok over high heat. Stir-fry scallops for 1 minute. Add radish and heat through. Add scallop liquid plus water, salt and wine. Cover and simmer for 10 minutes, until white radish is tender. Add dissolved cornstarch, stirring until thickened.

Abalone with Lettuce

4 servings

Ingredients:

½ head lettuce

7 oz. (200 g) canned abalone

2 tablespoons vegetable oil for frying

Seasonings:

    1 cup abalone liquid plus water or soup stock

    1 tablespoon Chinese rice wine or sake

    2–3 drops of sesame oil

    ½ teaspoon salt

    1 teaspoon cornstarch

Method:

1. Separate lettuce leaves. Rinse and drain. Slice abalone diagonally.

2. Heat 2 tablespoons vegetable oil in wok over high heat. Stir-fry lettuce for 1 minute, until soft. Add abalone and seasonings. Stir-fry for 1 minute, until thickened.

Crab with Cabbage

4 servings

Ingredients:

½ head Chinese cabbage
1 can crabmeat, about 7 oz. (200 g)
3 tablespoons vegetable oil for frying
1 green onion, chopped
1 fresh ginger, minced
1½ cups crabmeat liquid plus chicken soup
   stock
1 tablespoon Chinese rice wine or sake
⅔ teaspoon salt
1 teaspoon cornstarch, dissolved in
   2 tablespoons cold water

Method:

1. Cut Chinese cabbage lengthwise into ½-
   inch (1 cm) slices. Place in lightly salted
   boiling water. Cover and bring to a boil.
   Reduce heat and parboil 1–2 minutes, until
   soft. Drain.
2. Drain crabmeat and reserve liquid. Remove
   bones and flake crabmeat.
3. Heat 3 tablespoons vegetable oil in wok
   over high heat. Stir-fry green onion and
   ginger for 30 seconds. Add crabmeat and
   cabbage.
4. Add enough soup stock to crab liquid to
   make 1½ cups. Add to wok. Season with
   wine and salt. Simmer for 5 minutes, until
   cabbage is tender. Add dissolved cornstarch,
   stirring until thickened.

Creamed Chicken with Corn and Carrots

4 servings
Ingredients:
2 chicken wings
    1 teaspoon Chinese rice wine or sake
    ⅓ teaspoon salt
1 cup (145 g) diced carrot
1 cup (165 g) canned sweet corn, drained
2 tablespoons vegetable oil
⅓ teaspoon salt
1 teaspoon Chinese rice wine or sake
pepper
3 tablespoons evaporated milk
1 teaspoon cornstarch, dissolved in
    1 tablespoon cold water

Method:
1. Place chicken in boiling salted water and add wine. Cover and bring to a boil. Reduce heat and simmer for 1 minute, until meat is white. Drain liquid and reserve (about 2 cups).Parboil diced carrot in salted boiling water. Drain.

2. Heat 2 tablespoons vegetable oil in wok over high heat. Stir-fry carrot and corn for 3 minutes, until soft. Add chicken liquid. When the liquid has been reduced to only 20 % of its original amount, add salt, wine, pepper and evaporated milk. Add dissolved cornstarch, stirring until thickened.
3. Place chicken on serving platter. Pour corn-carrot sauce over chicken.

Cuttlefish with Celery

4 servings
Ingredients:
11 oz. (300 g) cuttlefish
4 stalks celery
1 carrot
3¼ oz. (100 g) canned mushrooms
3 tablespoons vegetable oil for frying
⅔ cup soup stock (see page 95)
1 tablespoon Chinese rice wine or sake
½ teaspoon salt
pepper
1 teaspoon cornstarch, dissolved in
   1 tablespoon cold water
½ teaspoon sesame oil

Method:
1. Rinse cuttlefish and remove skin. Cut the
    cuttlefish in half lengthwise. Score outside
    surface in a crisscross pattern, then cut into
    ½ × 2-inch (1.5 × 5 cm) pieces. Peel carrot
    and cut into ½ × 2-inch (1.5 × 5 cm) pieces.
    Cut mushrooms in half lengthwise.
2. Heat oil in wok over high heat. Stir-fry
    carrot for 2 minutes. Add celery, cuttlefish,
    and mushrooms. Stir-fry for 1 minute, until
    cuttlefish is white. Add soup, wine, salt and
    pepper. Add dissolved cornstarch, stirring
    until thickened. Sprinkle with sesame oil.

Egg and Vegetable Soup

4 servings

Ingredients:
4 fresh Chinese mushrooms
1 onion
15 snow pea pods
6 cups soup stock (see page 95)
1 tablespoon oil for stir-frying
⅔ teaspoon salt
1 tablespoon Chinese rice wine or sake
2 eggs, beaten
pepper
½ teaspoon sesame oil

Method:
1. Slice mushrooms and onion into thin pieces. Place snow pea pods in lightly salted boiling water. Cook for 10 minutes. Drain. Snap off and discard the ends.
2. Heat soup stock to boiling. Remove from heat.
3. Heat 1 tablespoon vegetable oil in wok over high heat. Stir-fry onion until tender. Add mushrooms, onion, salt, and wine.
4. Add vegetables to soup stock. Bring to a boil. Stir in beaten eggs and season with pepper and sesame oil. Garnish with snow peas.

Sautéed Pork with String Beans

4 servings

Ingredients:
10 oz. (300 g) string beans
2 oz. (70 g) dried bean threads
3 tablespoons oil
1 tablespoon minced fresh ginger
5 oz. (150 g) ground pork
2 tablespoons Chinese rice wine or sake
4 tablespoons soy sauce
2 tablespoons sugar
1 cup soup stock (see page 95)
½ teaspoon sesame oil

Method:
1. Wash the beans, snap off and discard the ends, and cut in half. Soak bean threads in lukewarm water for 10 minutes, until partly tender, drain and cut into 3-inch (8 cm) pieces.
2. Heat 3 tablespoons oil in wok over high heat for 1 minute. Stir-fry ginger. Add ground pork and stir-fry until meat is white.
3. Add string beans and stir-fry for 3 minutes. Add wine, soy sauce, sugar and soup stock. Simmer for 5 minutes until string beans are tender. Add bean threads. Sprinkle with sesame oil.

Scallop and Cucumber Salad

4 servings

Ingredients:

3 medium cucumbers
10 fresh scallops
2 teaspoons Chinese rice wine or sake
dash of salt
Dressing:
   1 teaspoon sugar
   1 tablespoon soy sauce
   2 teaspoons lemon juice
   2 teaspoons vegetable oil
   1 teaspoon sesame oil
   1 teaspoon fresh ginger juice
   ½ teaspoon mustard

Method:

1. Rub cucumbers with a little salt, wrap in plastic and refrigerate for 30 minutes.
2. Place scallops in wok, add water just to cover. Season with salt and Chinese rice wine. Bring to a boil and cook for 3 minutes. Drain and let cool in pan. Skin and devein scallops.
3. Combine dressing ingredients. Add scallops and marinate for 5 minutes.
4. Rinse cucumber, peel and cut into bite-size pieces.
5. Combine cucumbers with scallops. Serve cold.

Fried Rice with Vegetables

4 servings
Ingredients:
3 cups rice
1 chicken wing
2 teaspoons Chinese rice wine or sake
½ teaspoon salt
½ cup minced carrot
½ cup minced green pepper
½ cup minced celery
¼ cup minced green onion
3 tablespoons vegetable oil
salt
pepper
½ teaspoon sesame oil

Method:
1. Rinse rice and drain for 1 hour. Place in 3½ cups boiling water. Cover. Reduce heat and simmer for 25 minutes. Remove from heat, stir and let cool.
2. Place chicken on a plate and sprinkle with wine and salt. Place in hot steamer and steam for 7–8 minutes. Dice chicken finely.
3. Heat 3 tablespoons oil in wok over high heat. Stir-fry chicken for 30 seconds. Add rice, stir-fry thoroughly, and season with salt and pepper. Add vegetables. Stir-fry for 1 minute, until vegetables are mixed.

Snacks
Pictured on pages 62–63

Pearl Balls
Shao-mai
Pumpkin Dessert
Fried Shrimp Balls
Spring Rolls

Pearl Balls

4 servings

Ingredients:

½ cup glutinous rice (or barley grains)
2 dried Chinese mushrooms
10 oz. (300 g) ground pork
Seasonings:
  ½ onion, minced
  1 egg
  ½ teaspoon salt
  1 tablespoon Chinese rice wine or sake
  1 tablespoon cornstarch
  dash of pepper
sesame oil for greasing

Method:

1. Rinse rice thoroughly and soak in water for 6 hours. Drain and place in bowl.
2. Soak mushrooms in warm water for 30 minutes. Squeeze to drain well. Discard stems; mince mushrooms.
3. Combine pork and seasonings.

Knead well. Cover and refrigerate.

4. Shape pork mixture into 1-inch (2.5 cm) balls. Roll meatballs in rice.
5. Place meatballs in greased steamer over medium heat. Steam about 15 minutes.

Shao-Mai

Makes 30 (4 servings)
Ingredients:
Filling:
    3–4 dried Chinese mushrooms
    7 oz. (100 g) canned crabmeat, drained and
      boned
    10 oz. (300 g) ground pork
    1 egg
    ½ teaspoon salt
    dash of pepper
    ½ teaspoon sesame oil
    1 tablespoon vegetable oil
    1 tablespoon Chinese rice wine or sake
    1 onion, minced
    1 tablespoon cornstarch
30 shao-mai skins
oil for greasing

Method:
1. Soak mushrooms in warm water for 30 minutes. Squeeze to drain well. Discard stems; mince mushrooms.
2. Flake crabmeat in large pieces, reserving bright-colored portion for garnish.
3. Combine pork, egg, salt, pepper, sesame oil, vegetable oil and wine until sticky. Add onion, mushrooms and crabmeat and mix again. Add cornstarch.
4. Place about 1 tablespoon pork mixture in the middle of each shao-mai skin. Gather edges to wrap filling, garnish with reserved crabmeat.
5. Place shao-mai in hot greased steamer over high heat and steam for 12–13 minutes.

Pumpkin Dessert

4 servings

Ingredients:

14 oz. (400 g) fresh pumpkin
1 cup sugar
2 cups milk
½ teasoon almond extract
½ cup cornstarch
toasted and ground white sesame seeds for
  garnish

Method:

1. Pare, seed, and cut pumpkin into large
    pieces. Place in wok with sugar. Add boiling
    water to cover. Simmer for 25–30 minutes,
    until liquid has evaporated. Strain through
    sieve.
2. In pan, warm milk slightly, add cornstarch,
    almond extract and combine thoroughly.
    Bring to a boil, stirring constantly. Stir and
    boil for 2–3 minutes and add pumpkin.

3. Pour custard into greased 9 × 9-inch (22.5 ×
    22.5 cm) pan. Smooth the surface. Sprinkle
    with sesame seeds. Refrigerate.
4. Cut into pieces of desired size and place on
    serving plate.

Fried Shrimp Balls

4 servings

Ingredients:

7 oz. (200 g) shelled shrimp
2 oz. (70 g) pork fat
1 teaspoon ginger juice
½ teaspoon salt
1 teaspoon Chinese rice wine or sake
1 egg white
1 tablespoon cornstarch
2–3 slices of thin-sliced bread
5 cups oil for deep-drying

Method:

1. Devein shrimp. Chop and pound with the sharp side of a knife until it becomes a paste. Mince fat.
2. In bowl, combine shrimp paste, fat, ginger juice, salt, wine, and egg white. Add cornstarch and knead thoroughly. Shape into 1-inch (2.5 cm) balls.
3. Dice sliced bread into ¼-inch (6 mm) cubes.
4. Roll shrimp balls in bread cubes.
5. Heat 5 cups vegetable oil in wok over medium heat. Deep-fry shrimp balls for 2–3 minutes, turning often to make evenly golden brown.

Spring Rolls

4 servings (10 rolls)
Ingredients:
Filling:
  3 dried Chinese mushrooms
  1 chicken wing
  2 teaspoons Chinese rice wine or sake
  ½ stalk clery
  ½ carrot
  2 green peppers
  2 Chinese cabbage leaves
  3½ oz. (100 g) fresh bean sprouts
10 spring roll wrappers
Seasonings:
  ½ teaspoon salt
  pepper
  ½ teaspoon sesame oil
  ½ tablespoon Chinese rice wine or sake
  ¼ teaspoon sugar
2 tablespoons cornstarch, dissolved in 4 teaspoons cold water
3 tablespoons vegetable oil
5 cups vegetable oil for deep-frying

Method:
1. Soak mushrooms in warm water for 30 minutes. Squeeze to drain well. Discard stems; cut mushrooms into thin strips.
2. Place chicken on a plate. Sprinkle with wine. Place plate in steamer. Steam over high heat for 20 minutes. Remove bones and shred meat. Cut celery, carrot, green peppers and Chinese cabbage stems into thin strips. Rinse bean sprouts and drain.
3. Separate spring roll wrappers. Cover with damp cloth to keep moist.
4. Heat 3 tablespoons vegetable oil in wok and stir-fry mushrooms. Add remaining filling ingredients and seasonings. Stir-fry quickly. Stir in dissolved cornstarch until thickened. Cool.
5. Place one tenth of the filling on each wrapper. Roll diagonally. Fold in ends. Fold over top point and seal by brushing edges with flour paste.
6. Heat 5 cups vegetable oil in wok over high heat to 360°F. (180°C.). Deep-fry spring rolls for 3 minutes, turning occasionally, until evenly golden brown.

Almond Jelly

4 servings
Ingredients:
1 stick *kanten* (agar-agar)
3 cups cold water
1 cup sugar
1 cup milk
½ teaspoon almond extract
melon (cantaloupe or muskmelon) or straw-
    berries

Method:
1. Soak *kanten* in cold water about 1 hour, changing water several times. Squeeze to drain well. Tear into small pieces.
2. Boil 3 cups cold water and add *kanten*. Stir until completely dissolved.
3. Stir in sugar. When dissolved, remove from heat and add milk and almond extract.
4. Strain through gauze and pour into indi- vidual serving molds. Let cool in refrig- erator.
5. **Pare and seed melon; cut into large pieces.** Purée in blender. If using strawberries, wash thoroughly and remove stems before blend- ing.
6. When jelly has set, pour melon or straw- berry purée over jelly and serve.

Sesame Custard Cakes

4 servings

Ingredients:

1/2 cup flour, sifted
2 tablespoons cornstarch
4 tablespoons sugar
2 cups milk
2 egg yolks, beaten
3 tablespoons cornstarch for dusting
5 cups vegetable oil for deep-frying
Coating:
    4 tablespoons white sesame seeds, toasted
      and ground
    4 tablespoons sugar

Method:

1. Combine flour, cornstarch, sugar, and half of the milk. Add the remaining milk and beat until smooth.
2. Cook custard over medium heat, stirring until thick. Reduce heat, add egg yolks and mix thoroughly. When custard becomes very sticky, remove from heat.
3. Lightly dust flat pan with cornstarch and pour in custard. Smooth surface of custard and lightly dust with cornstarch. Let cool thoroughly and cut into 1 × 3-inch (2.5 × 7.5 cm) strips.
4. Heat 5 cups vegetable oil in wok over high heat. Deep-fry custard strips for 1 minute, until lightly brown. Drain on paper towels.
6. Roll custard strips in coating.

Quick & Easy Recipes

Sweet and Sour Pork

Ingredients:

11 oz. (300 g) pork fillet, cut into bite-size pieces
Seasonings:
    1½ teaspoons soy sauce
    1 teaspoon Chinese rice wine or sake
    1 teaspoon vegetable oil
    dash of pepper
    1 tablespoon cornstarch
2 cups vegetable oil for frying meat
2–3 medium green peppers, cut into bite-size
    pieces
3 tablespoons vegetable oil for stir-frying
4 canned pineapple slices, cut into bite-size pieces
salt
pepper
2 teaspoons Chinese rice wine or sake

Method:

1. Combine seasonings in bowl; stir until thickened. Add pork and stir to coat evenly. Marinate for 15 minutes.
2. Heat 2 cups vegetable oil in wok over medi-um-low heat. Stir-fry pork for 10 seconds, and green pepper for 4 seconds. Remove pork and green peper. Drain oil from wok.
3. Heat 3 tablespoons vegetable oil in wok over high heat. Stir-fry pineapple for 4 seconds. Add pork, green pepper, wine, salt and pepper. Stir-fry to heat through.

Pork with Chinese Mushrooms

4 servings

Ingredients:

7 oz. (200 g) pork ham, cut into bite-size pieces
Seasonings:
    1½ teaspoons Chinese rice wine or sake
    1–2 teaspoons soy sauce
    1–2 teaspoons cornstarch
3–4 dried Chinese mushrooms
green vegetable (mustard greens or
    ching-kêng-ts'ai)
3½ oz. (100 g) cooked bamboo shoots
3–4 fresh ginger slices
3–4 green onion slices
2 cups vegetable oil for frying pork
3 tablespoons vegetable oil for stir-frying
1 tablespoon Chinese rice wine or sake
½ teaspoon salt
pepper
sesame oil

Method:

1. Combine seasonings in bowl; stir until thickened. Add pork and stir to coat evenly.
2. Soak mushrooms in lukewarm water for 30 minutes. Squeeze to drain well. Discard stems; cut mushrooms diagonally into 2-inch (5 cm) slices.
3. Cook green vegetable in lightly salted boiling water until color changes. Cut into 2-inch (5 cm) lengths.
4. Cut bamboo shoots into thin slices. Cut green onion diagonally into 1-inch (3 cm) slices.
5. Heat 2 cups vegetable oil in wok over medium-low heat. Deep-fry pork for 2 minutes, until meat is white. Remove pork. Drain oil from wok.
6. Heat 3 tablespoons vegetable oil in wok over high heat. Stir-fry green onions and ginger for 10 seconds. Add green vegetables, mushrooms and bamboo shoots. Stir-fry for 3–5 seconds. Add pork, wine and salt. Stir-fry to heat through. Sprinkle with pepper and sesame oil.

Soup with Meatballs and Chrysanthemum Leaves

4 servings
Ingredients:
Meatballs:
  ⅔ lb. (300 g) ground pork
  1 green onion, minced
  4–5 dried Chinese musrooms
  1 egg
  1½ tablespoons Chinese rice wine or sake
  1 tablespoon cornstarch
  dash of pepper
  ¼ teaspoon salt
  ¼ teaspoon sesame oil
Soup:
  3–4 cups soup stock (see page 95)
  1 tablespoon Chinese rice wine or sake
  ½ teaspoon salt
½ bunch chrysanthemum leaves (*shun-giku*)
1 tablespoon cornstarch dissolved in 2
  tablespoons cold water
salt

pepper
sesame oil

Method:
1. Soak mushrooms in cold water for 1 hour. Squeeze to drain well. Discard stems; chop mushrooms.
2. Combine meatball ingredients and knead well. Shape into ½-inch (1.5 cm) balls.
3. Bring soup stock to a boil. Stir in wine and salt. Add meatballs. Return to a boil. Reduce heat and simmer for 5 minutes. Skim off any fat that may rise to the surface.
4. Cut off and discard root ends of chrysanthemum leaves. Slice into 1-inch (2 cm) lengths and add to soup. Add cornstarch mixture, stirring until thickened. Sprinkle with salt, pepper and sesame oil.

Deep-Fried Chicken in Three-Nut Batter

4 servings

Ingredients:

7 oz. (200 g) chicken breasts, boned
Seasonings:
   2 teaspoons Chinese rice wine or sake
   ¼ teaspoon salt
   dash of pepper
3½ oz. (100 g) walnuts, coarsely chopped
3½ oz. (100 g) pine nuts, coarsely chopped
3½ oz. (100 g) cashew nuts, coarsely chopped
2 egg whites
2 teaspoons cornstarch
5 cups vegetable oil for deep-frying
4 sprigs parsley

Method:

1. Cut chicken breasts diagonally into three pieces. Combine with seasonings. Set aside.
2. Beat egg whites lightly. Stir in cornstarch to make a batter. Combine chopped nuts in a shallow dish. Dip chicken in batter and then in nuts.
3. Heat 5 cups vegetable oil in wok over medium heat. Deep-fry chicken for 3 minutes, turning occasionally, until golden brown.
4. Arrange on serving platter. Garnish with parsley.

Deep-fried Stuffed Peppers

4 servings

Ingredients:

½ lb. (250 g) ground pork
Vegetables, minced:
  3–4 dried Chinese mushrooms
  1 green onion
  2 oz. (50 g) boiled fresh bamboo shoots
  (or canned)
¼ teaspoon salt
dash of pepper
1½ teaspoons Chinese rice wine or sake
½ teaspoon sesame oil
1 egg white
1½ teaspoons cornstarch
5–6 medium green peppers
cornstarch for coating
4 cups vegetable oil for deep-frying

Method:

1. Soak mushrooms in lukewarm water for
   30 minutes. Squeeze to drain well. Discard
   stems; mince mushrooms.

2. Combine ground pork, minced vegetables,
   salt, pepper, wine and sesame oil. Knead
   well. Add egg white and cornstarch. Knead
   again.
3. Cut green peppers in half lengthwise. Remove seeds and membranes. Sprinkle inside
   surfaces with cornstarch to coat. Stuff with
   pork mixture to form a smooth mound.
4. Heat vegetable oil in wok to 338°F. (170°C.).
   Place green peppers in oil with meat-side
   down. Deep-fry, turning occasionally, until
   meat is browned.
5. Serve with mustard and soy sauce.

Shredded Chicken with Chinese Pickles

Variation: Use cucumber in place of Chinese pickles. Slice into thin strips and sprinke with salt. Let stand for 30 minutes. Drain completely.

4 servings

Ingredients:

1 steamed chicken thigh, see recipe page 44
3–4 Chinese pickles
(*cha-ts'ai* or pickled mustard greens)
Seasonings:
2 teaspoons soy sauce
2 teaspoons vinegar
1 teaspoon sesame oil

Method:

1. Prepare steamed chicken as on page 44, steps 1–5. Remove bones. Cut into thin strips.
2. Rinse Chinese pickles. Cut into thin strips. Soak in water for 10 minutes to remove salt. Squeeze to drain completely.
3. Combine chicken and pickles in a bowl. Add seasonings. Mix well. Serve cold.

See photo on the back cover

Fried Chicken Wings

4 servings
Ingredients:
15 chicken wings
Marinade:
    4½ teaspoons Chinese rice wine or sake
    ¼ cup soy sauce
    1 tablespoon sugar
    1½ teaspoon sesame oil
    4 sliced ginger
    ½ green onions, sliced
    1 clove garlic, crushed
    10 peppercorns
5 cups vegetable oil for deep-frying
¼ head cabbage, shredded
1 tomato

Method:
1. Combine marinade ingredients. Marinate chicken wings for 1 hour.
2. Dry chicken on paper towels.
3. Heat 5 cups vegetable oil in wok over medium heat. Fry wings for 3 minutes, turning occasionally. Remove chicken. Raise heat to high. Re-fry chicken for 10 seconds until golden brown and crisp.
4. Arrange chicken on serving platter around a nest of shredded cabbage.
5. Wash tomato. Remove stem. Cut almost through to form 6 sections. Gently peel the skin from each section. Fold out skin to resemble flower petals. Place tomato flower in center of cabbage nest.

Chicken Soup Stock

Makes 6–11 cups
Ingredients:
2–3 (2 lb. or 1 kg) bony chicken parts; neck, back, wing, foot
3–4 green onions, cut in half
1 fresh ginger root, crushed
3½ qt. (4 l) water; about 17 cups

Method:
1. Cut chicken parts into pieces. Rinse in water.
2. Bring some water to a boil. Add chicken and boil for 3–4 minutes, until meat is white and tender. Remove chicken and rinse in water. Crush ginger with dull edge of knife.
3. Place chicken, green onion and ginger in 3½ qt. (4 l) water. Cover; bring to a boil. Reduce heat and simmer for 2 to 2½ hours.
4. Skim off any fat that may rise to surface. Strain soup.
Storage: Stock may be kept in the refrigerator up to 1 week, or in the freezer for 2 months.

Typical Chinese Seasonings

Although Chinese cooking does make much use of such typically Japanese ingredients as soy sauce and sake, there are certain other seasonings that are more distinctly Chinese.
Oyster sauce, made from crushed oysters, has a salty flavor like the soy sauce with which it is made. A light sprinkling of sesame oil, added just before serving, adds flavor and lustar. **Hot brown bean paste** (*tou-pan-chiang*) flavored with red peppers, added at the stove or at the table, has a sharp, hot-spicy taste.

Dried Ingredients for Soup

Dried ingredients, including scallops, shrimp, mushroom, are a common feature of Chinese cooking. They are used in soup stocks, fried dishes, and many other recipes. To prepare: rinse in water, add hot water just to cover, cover and let stand overnight.

Dried Scallops

Choose large, shiny, amber-colored scallops. Reserve water in which they are soaked and use in recipe.

Dried Shrimp

Remove shell. Dry meat. Choose shrimp that have good flavor.

Dried Mushrooms

Look for mushrooms with thick tops. Avoid those with yellowish undersides because they are less flavorful.

How to Cut a Whole Chicken

1. Cut chicken in half lengthwise. **(1)**
2. To remove legs, cut the skin between leg and body. Lift leg until hip is free from body. Cut between hip joint and body, close to body. Cut leg into bite-size pieces. To remove wings, cut at the inside of the wing, just above the joint. **(2–3)**
3. Slice the body into thin strips.

Seasonings for Fried Dishes

Star anise (*pa-chiao*) is commonly used to season pork and giblets. **Cloves** and **cinnamon** are other popular spices. **Five-spice powder** (*wu-hsiang-fên*) is a blend of star anise, cloves, cinnamon and fennel. It is best to use a light touch when adding spices.

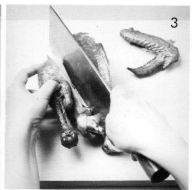

Index of Recipes